FIRETHORNE
The Gustavus Journal of Literary and Graphic Arts

SPRING 2015
GUSTAVUS ADOLPHUS COLLEGE

FIRETHORNE SUBMISSION POLICY

Firethorne is Gustavus Adolphus College's student-run literary magazine comprised solely of student work. *Firethorne* is published twice a year, with a supplemental in the fall and a full-length publication in the spring.

Students may submit their work by emailing firethorne@gustavus.edu with "*Firethorne* Submission" in the subject line and the student's name, year, and major included in the body of the email. Emails must attach prose and poetry in Microsoft Word format in a standard font without color (Times New Roman, 12 pt.). Attachment file names should reflect the titles of the work you are submitting and the student's name should not be included anywhere in the document itself. Artwork and photography must be sent as a JPEG file with reasonable file compression (300-600 dpi), again with the file name reflecting the title of the piece. Multiple submissions should be sent as separate attachments. Drawings/paintings/etc. that are being submitted may either be scanned and then emailed, or can be a high quality physical copy. *Firethorne* encourages collaboration between artistis and photographers; pictures of sculpture and other multimedia works will be credited to both their creators and photographers. Physical copies of paper artwork can be submitted through the Gustavus Adolphus post office and sent to Professor Baker Lawley. *Firethorne* will not publish anonymous work or materials submitted from a non-Gustavus email address.

The Managing Editor will systematically code all submitted work and turn over the submitted work, without attribution, for the editors' scrutiny. *Firethorne* staff will admit submissions for creativity, originality and artistic value.

For prose, submissions should be 2500 words or less. Artwork and photography can be color and up to any size, however please take note that color may be cost prohibitive depending on available funds. In this event, *Firethorne* staff will convert artwork to grayscale with the submitter's consent.

Submissions marked for publication will appear in their original submitted form except for technical aspects such as font, size, page placement and corrections of obvious grammatical errors. Stylistic changes (i.e. word substitutions, changes in length of the work, word omissions, etc.) recommended by the editors will be made only with the submitter's consent. If recommended changes are not approved by the submitter, they will not be made; however the publication of the work will then be determined by the *Firethorne* staff as it reflects our artistic mission for the publication as a whole. It is against *Firethorne* policy to publish works that do not reflect the submitter's artistic integrity.

Firethorne will publish up to two works from an individual student in each issue, except in special cases when issue space may require more. This policy is applicable to both *Firethorne* editors and the general student body. Staff members' works will undergo the editing process like all other submissions.

The views and/or opinions expressed in the publication are not to be taken as those of *Firethorne* staff or its associated bodies. Materials deemed to place the publication at risk for liability with regard to obscenity or profanity in connection with hate speech, slander or other illegal forms of speech will be removed at the staff's discretion. Work found to be fraudulent in nature or plagiarized will be disqualified upon confirmation.

Inquiries into *Firethorne* can be made by contacting:
Baker Lawley, Associate Professor of English, *Firethorne* Advisor
blawley@gustavus.edu
507-933-7402
http://orgs.gustavus.edu/firethorne
This policy was revised September 2012. *Firethorne*, MMXII all rights reserved.

Acknowledgments

The Spring 2015 *Firethorne* Editors would like to offer our deepest gratitude to the following people, without whom this publication would not have been possible:

Gustavus Department of English and the Gustavus Student Senate, for their generous financial support;

Jenny Tollefson, for her administrative direction;

Baker Lawley, our faculty advisor, for his support in pursuing self-publishing, and for his knowledge and encouragement;

our section editors for the leadership and dedication, and the rest of our editors for lending their time and their minds to this publication;

the talented Gustavus students who submitted their work for consideration;

and to you, our valued readers, for your interest in and passion for the written word and artistic expression.

Thank you,
The Firethorne Editors

LETTER FROM THE EDITORS

Dear Reader,

Thank you for investing your time in this spring issue of Firethorne. A publication like this would not be possible without the support and contributions of the Gustavus community. The printed word continues to influence readers even in our increasingly digital society.

We hope you enjoy reading and considering the many ideas presented here. We are of course dependent on submissions for this journal and appreciate that each semester the distribution of artistic works varies, yet functions as a whole. This spring we had a multitude of art submissions which we felt we could include more of to make this issue wonderfully visual in nature.

To our fellow editors who worked with us on this issue, thank you for your commitment. It is an honor to collaborate with you on such a publication.

Sincerely,

Elizabeth Lutz & Laura Isdahl

FIRETHORNE STAFF

MANAGING EDITOR
Elizabeth Lutz

ORGANIZATIONAL MANAGER
Laura Isdahl

LAYOUT EDITORS
Thi Hoang
Melissa Saholt

PROMOTIONS ASSISTANT
Erika Clifton

PROSE SECTION EDITOR
Molly Butler

PROSE EDITORS
Emma Hunt   Melissa Saholt
August Jasnoch   Kelsey Skjerping
Jack Poblocki   Sydney Seewald

POETRY SECTION EDITOR
Aaron Lawrence

POETRY EDITORS
Grace Bymark   Emma Schmidtke
Kjerstin Piper

ART SECTION EDITOR
Blake Van Oosbree

ART EDITORS
Erika Clifton   Carly Maslowski

Table of Contents

Prose

Nels Foslien	09	Sonder is a Made-Up Word: A True Story
Molly Butler	14	The Pit
Tara Robinson	22	A Fork in the Road
Dylan Jensen	28	Little Masters

Art

Tyler Brower	30	Hassan and Goat
	32	Street Market
	34	Arabian Desert Saudi Arabia
	36	Sa'ad
	38	Syrian Refugees
Blake Van Oosbree	40	Expression
Katie Feterl	42	Landmannalauger
Caleb Merritt	44	Let This Be Your Sanctuary
	46	Pillar of Salt, Water
Lily Benge Briggs	48	Orchard Basket
Aimee Cichon	50	Serenity
Meishon Behboudi	52	Solace
	54	Sundar
Sage Macklay	56	Star-Nosed Mole
Elizabeth Lutz	58	Alan
	60	Three Hundred Years From Now
Lesley Darling	62	Daniel's Reading
	64	Fog on Bay (Three Friends Laughing)
	66	Water in Three Forms

POETRY

Sophie Panetti	**69**	Blood on the Tracks
Nick Kowalski	**70**	In the First Degree
Judith Gabriel	**71**	They're Wearing My Shirts
Greg Meyer	**72**	If I Got A Tatoo
Joel Stremmel	**73**	Ode to Nick Drake
Mia Cannon	**74**	Installed 3/1/14
Elizabeth Lutz	**75**	My Bee Brother
	76	Hemlocks

Cover Art: "Fog on Bay (Chiseled Rock)" by Lesley Darling, Senior Scandinavian Studies Major

Cover Quotation: from "Ode to Nick Drake" by Joel Stemmel, Junior Math & Philosophy Major

Sonder is a Made-up Word: A True Story

"I don't feel comfortable driving in this anymore."

Reina and I were driving through Wyoming on the way back from a ski trip in Utah. It had been a hot day and the snow by the side of the road had melted and now was freezing again in the sun's absence.

"There's a town a few miles ahead," I said, poking through the GPS. "It's called Douglas. We can stop there for the night."

We had planned on driving a few more hours tonight, so pulling over meant an extra-long haul tomorrow.

Reina and I are on the ski team so we're used to staying in hotels all over the West and Midwest. We know what to look for in hotels. The best hotel we had stayed at had a heated swimming pool on the roof and served S'mores from 8 to 10 pm on the shore of Lake Superior. The worst had tried to charge us an extra $1.50 for not using the thoughtfully provided safe. We had to insist they take it off the bill.

The first hotel we tried was in a new development. In the lobby, it had shiny countertops and a shiny-faced clerk. It had a stone fireplace and white tile floor. It had fresh potted plants and black leather chairs. It was completely booked for the night.

The second hotel was in the shadow of the first. It seemed to be a smaller version. A little sister, perhaps. The clerk was smoking a cigarette outside the entrance. It was also booked. We figured it must be the roads.

We had to settle for the third hotel. The third was a sprawling old hotel at the edge of town. A white rectangle sign presented it as "The Douglas Inn" in Times New Roman. The lobby was massive with a great brick fireplace in the center and a pool at the far end. The floor was carpeted with musty hexagons and the walls were scattered with the heads and hides of various animals, which added to the western theme, I supposed. It had once been a place of grandeur. Off to the left was a small desk behind which a young woman sat typing. She wore a thin skirt and a half-untucked button up. One strand of brown hair had escaped her bun.

She looked up as we approached, offering a forced smile.

"Hi, checking in?"

Her nametag indicated "Katy"; it was slightly askew. She couldn't read my driver's license and had to ask for my name three times.

"Nels. N-E-L-S."

Katy was fidgety, as though our presence made her uncomfortable. She kept forgetting exactly what paper work was needed. As I filled in my license plate number, her friend walked in—just to visit.

Katy did not greet her friend, nor give any warning or sign of acknowledgement. She merely looked up at her, her dark eyes staring, evoking all the pain of a hotel clerk nearing the end of a long working weekend.

"We lost custody," said Katy, blankly.

A *very* long weekend.

I scratched a couple of my initials across the paper as the hotel clerk continued her story.

"…I filed a restraining order…"

I began to sign the bottom. *N-E-L-S.*

"…My whole life went to complete shit in one weekend."

I rounded the last curve on my signature. The ink sank into the white paper and dried.

The two women hugged, seeming to forget that Reina and I existed. We slipped off to our room as Katy stated detachedly, "*I don't feel safe anymore.*"

The best hotels leave out hot chocolate at all times and Reina and I usually love to wander down to the lobby late at night for a cup, but tonight was different. We stayed in our room preferring card games and Wyoming public television to risking any more encounters with the locals.

We went to bed earlier than usual in anticipation of the long drive ahead of us, but it was a vain attempt. I had just began to feel the first tendrils of sleep closing in on me and—

Bang. Bang. Bang.

Someone was pounding on our door. I jumped awake, heart pounding against its cage.

I rolled over to glance at the clock. 2:13 am.

Bang. Bang. Bang.

The knocking was relentless, growing in volume and vigor. Reina and I stared at each other in the darkness, our tangle-haired outlines. Sleep rapidly evaporated from our eyes.

Bang. Bang. Bang.

We were in the middle of Wyoming. Nowhere. 700 miles from anyone we knew.

Bang. Bang. Bang. Bang.

"Don't open it," she mouthed, as if I was going to.

Eventually the pounding stopped, only to resume again on the next door down the hall. Then the one after.

Reina collapsed back on her bed and I, too, closed my eyes, still keeping one ear tuned to the pounding in the hall.

Then the shouting began.

"Leave us alone!" A woman. It might have been Katy. We strained to follow the conversation.

"I found you—I fucking found you!" A man—evidently the one who had been knocking on doors.

"It's none of your business what we do!" The woman again.

"I'll knock on every damn door in this hotel if I have to. You've already made me a fool! You can't leave me out here like this!"

"It's over! It's over!"

"I'll kill you! I'll kill myself!"

Reina and I looked at each other. *Should we call 911? Should we call the front desk?* Wordlessly, we agreed it was better not to get involved.

Even as they left, I lay, staring at the ceiling, reflecting. I drifted through sonder as though I was drifting slowly through empty space. In another world, a woman needed help. Or maybe it was the man. Or neither. Maybe they could solve the problem themselves. Albeit publicly. It would only take me a few seconds to walk a dozen feet to the door, open it. But then the seal would be broken, there was no going back.

It's a strange concept—to intervene. To violently insert yourself into a stranger's life. How can I, as an outsider, make a difference, when I don't fully understand the problem? When I had never even been to this town before?

Suppose I did open the door. What would I say? What would I do? Would they listen to me? Would they attack me?

That was the other concern. The man had already threatened to kill someone. The most violently arguing couples have been known to unite if only to fend off a well-meaning outsider, then resume—isn't that Stockholm syndrome? And with these roads there was nowhere for me to run. Reina and I had made the right decision. Self-preservation came before all else. I don't think Reina had even questioned it.

I rolled over and buried my face in my pillow. It was a long night.

The next morning we ate breakfast and left in a hurry. The hotel was empty except for a posse of young men with sausage pan belt buckles standing in the lobby. They watched us silently with hooded eyes. The eggs were overcooked.

MOLLY BUTLER - *JUNIOR*
ENGLISH MAJOR

The Pit

Leah Rotto was not the most fortunate person, but as she plummeted down thirteen feet of empty air into the earth, she thought no one had ever looked so pitiful. Her limbs drifted. Her elbows scraped the rocky walls. A seam of her backpack tore open like a wound. There was a delicate crack as her ankle fractured on impact. Then Leah sat, legs crumpled beneath her, at the bottom of the pit.

The hole was in the field near the small woods of the campus arboretum. Its source was unknown, and it served sometimes as a meeting place for joints to be passed round, or a garbage disposal for passersby. Lays potato chip bags, dull bits of glass from drunken evenings, a somber purple condom wrapper, ashes from cigarettes and joints, a single sheet of notebook paper with notes written in bubbly handwriting on the anthropological interests of Hmong culture, leaves fallen from the nearby woods. All these things peered at Leah dreamily in the gloom. The narrow opening of the hole choked most of the afternoon sunlight.

Leah tenderly slid her backpack from her arms, pulled it to her side and rested her back directly on the dirt wall. It was cool down here in the darkness. The smell of damp, earthy life was nearly overwhelming.

The smell of damp bodies, cologne, and beer was overwhelming. Bodies crammed wall to wall and Ke$ha chanted over blown out speakers. Upstairs joints were being passed round and round. Downstairs the living room couches were being trampled by gyrating girls, sticking their tongues out to the lyrics. Ping-pong balls sailed over a cracked wooden board. Nothing below a scream could be heard. The walls began to sweat.

Leah clutched a warm Coors and tried to find something to lean against. The space between her skirt and boots felt bare. Sweat was sliding down her back. Leah wondered if she had drunk too much or not enough. She sipped warm beer.

"Hey Leah, hey how are you?" a guy from Chemistry, with the mole on his throat, what's his name, everyone looks so different out of class, so different at parties.

"Hey," she managed, trying not to lean on things, trying to forget the sweat collecting in her bra.

"Hey, how are you? Havin' fun? Hey, I haven't seen you here," he was all grins.

"Yeah, Chelsea invited me," she tried more beer.

"Hey, it's good to see you. Didn't think I'd ever see you out. Hey, how'd you do on the lab? A real bitch, ya know. Hey, wanna be pong partners? These guys are headin' out," a hand on her waist lead her through the steaming room. The table stretched before them. Swear words had been carved on every inch. Leah set her empty beer can next to an etching which claimed "Jake is a thot."

"Hey, you outta beer? Have one of mine," a fresh beer appeared in her hand. "Hey Leah, you ready to go?" he took her hand and put a pong ball in it. He was all grins. She returned a smile, pushing a hand through her hair, trying to tug the sweaty strands from her damp face and neck. She missed most of the shots and drank two beers but that was okay. Her throat felt dry and Ke$ha started to sound good.

Leah began assessing the situation she'd fallen into. Small trickles of blood oozed from the scrapes on both elbows, her jeans were damp from the dirt floor, and her left ankle had begun to bruise. Though her backpack had torn along one seem, the contents had remained inside.

"Well fuck," Leah whispered at nothing.

Time became a strange factor in the bottom of a hole, where the world didn't seem to spin. Leah's cell phone was sitting face down on her desk in the dorm. Leah didn't carry a watch.

"Down the rabbit hole," she thought. After two years at college studying things like Freud and mythology and what Shakespeare meant when he said carrot, Leah entertained herself with notions of symbolism. Her mind idled on images of falling. Icarus and Alice. They crashed. The world spun in strange directions these days. Leah had grown accustomed to feeling unsteady on her feet.

Leah realized her throat was dry. There were two bottles, one tucked into each side of her backpack. One was her water bottle, two thirds full. The other was a generous half and half mix of Gatorade and ten dollar vodka Leah had added that morning.

"Drink me." She almost smiled. She took the bottle filled with water and drank.

"I think I drank t'much," Leah slurred. Her sinuses burned with the vomit she had narrowly missed spewing on the bed. Sprawled on her stomach, head dangling over the edge, she half heartedly aimed at the garbage bucket. The dried gum stuck to the bottom disappeared under a layer of watery, yellow puke. The edges of Leah's vision were blurring. She peered at a poster of a frazzled Einstein on the wall, and her stomach churned as the room swayed. Einstein watched as fresh vomit splattered into the bucket.

"Hey, c'mere, you alright? Feelin' good?"

"Where we," Leah panted and tried to curl up.

"Hey, hey, c'mere," a hand stroking her arm, idling on her hip. Leah shivered and shook and drooled a strand of stomach acid onto the bed.

"Come over here Leah," more firmly now. The hand, on her elbow, a tug.

"Where we," Leah repeated, swaying between the oncoming blackness and a fresh wave of nausea.

"Hey, it's me. Hey, c'mere Leah," the hand was on her elbow. Leah tried to curl up and wondered if she looked worse than Einstein and where Chelsea was and how big the space was between her boots and her skirt.

"Where're we," Leah moaned.

"Hey," he said. Leah couldn't see if he was grinning.

Leah didn't drink much water. Every survivalist fiction she'd laid her hands on in elementary school said you're supposed to conserve that. Besides, once the sun had gone down and the temperature dropped, the bottle labeled Gatorade became far more appealing.

The vodka mix was harsh and welcome. Each sip made her shudder involuntarily. Leah hadn't eaten since she had pushed scrambled eggs around a plate at breakfast, and the initial sip sent woozy warmth to her limbs. Knowing that these rations were precious, she drank just enough to mute the pain in her ankle and warm her feeble limbs. Drinking slowly in the darkness of the night, and blackness of the pit, Leah wondered if it was cloudy or if the sky was sprinkled with stars. She never bothered to look up.

After some time, there was no way to know how much, she pulled her arms into her shirt and slid lazily onto her side. Bits of glass and rock poked her side but her buzz kept these sensations distant. She rested her head on her backpack and braced herself for dreams.

"Well was he any fun?" Chelsea's voice was flat on the phone. A few streaks of afternoon sun had snuck past the closed curtains and were drawing golden lines on the walls. Leah was sitting on the floor of her dorm, facing her floor length mirror. She hadn't managed to scrub off all the mascara from her face. At this angle her face was distorted, alien in the mirror.

"I.." Leah's fingers plucked at her elbows. "He…" Leah tried again but her voice cracked.

"Leah, what the hell," Chelsea was bored.

"I…It. I dunno what happened,"

"Oh my god Leah, you must have been plastered," Chelsea was gleeful.

"Yeah," Leah closed her eyes.

"I feel ya girl," Chelsea was picking up speed. "I was still drunk when I left this morning, I swear to god I almost puked, I'm so glad you came out last night with me finally, did you see Rachel with

Tommy what the fucking hell," Leah listened to the sounds rather than the words, not meeting her own eyes.

"So are you coming out again tonight?" Chelsea asked abruptly.

"No. I...I hafta. Recover."

"Okay girl well I gotta go I need a nap mkay call me if you change your mind buh-bye." Leah let the phone fall into the cradle of her sweatshirt. Then, because there was nothing else to be done, Leah let herself fall slowly onto her side and lay curled on the floor, waiting. Salty tears licked the mascara on her cheeks.

Leah's neck was stiff when she woke up in the pit, birds chirping in the hazy yellow light above. Her ankle had sprouted a massive bruise with a foul tint of green. The whole ordeal puffed over her sneakers. She wriggled herself upright.

"Doc told me to get out more," Leah thought, and almost smiled. Almost. The earth at the bottom of the hole was firm from the cold, but maintained a smell of life, or maybe decaying life. Leah began to wonder about real rabbit holes, about gophers curled up in fluffy beds just feet away, the busy network of worms and beetles and tree roots squirming all around her. She thought underground things were more alive than the things above.

The early bird gets worms, where on earth but six feet under, dirt cheap and clear as mud. Broken idioms and phrases plodded through Leah's tired mind, the mechanics of her brain spinning away incessantly while she idly watched.

"Doc told me to get outside more," Leah muttered aloud this time. Her voice sounded like she had smoked for years. Unintelligible thoughts persisted while Leah stared at the dirt surrounding her.

Doctor Tabilorse was seated on the couch with one leg crossed, a patch of hairy ankle exposed. His eyebrows were raised to incredible heights in an attempt to make his eyes appear more understanding.

"How is your diet? It's important to get vitamin B. It is excellent at fighting depression you know," Doctor Tabilorse's voice was so soothing. Leah wondered how many days it had been since she'd eaten. Her stomach felt like it was going to overflow with acid. Her tongue had forgotten how to taste.

"No, I don't think I'm getting my vitamins," she had not felt so talkative in weeks. She needed to be more proactive. It was her fault she wasn't getting better. A burning coal was warming her numb chest, something she vaguely recognized as frustration, maybe anger. She'd brought an elephant to this room and too late realized it was her responsibility to quietly remove it. Doctor Tabilorse sighed.

"I don't like to do this, but since my other suggestions have apparently not produced results," an undeniable tone of sarcasm. "I'm writing you a prescription for Clonazepam. A benzodiazapine. It's habit forming, so just one at a time, only when you feel an attack of anxiety. Fast acting. Try taking just half a pill the first time." Doctor Tabilorse scribbled on a pad. He tore off the prescription and handed it to Leah.

"We'll try that and you let me know how that works when we meet next month," Doctor Tabilorse was standing up. Leah rose. "In the mean time, try to get some vitamin B, along with some exercise for the endorphins. It's going to be nice out soon, try getting outside," Doctor Tabilorse was opening the door. Leah picked up her bag and headed into the hallway.

"Make another appointment with Linda at the front desk," Doctor Tabilorse closed the door to his office. Leah stood, clutching her bag and the prescription, feeling toxic. She left Plymouth Psychiatric Clinic without stopping at the desk.

Her latest refill of Clonazepam still had seven pills in it. Leah fished it out of the bottom of her backpack with cold fingers. It took most of her strength to pry the white cap off the bottle. She dumped two round white pills into her trembling palm. Somewhere on the surface she heard voices, a class walking by, Ecology or Botany, looking at trees, long legged girls, boys clutching their notebooks like footballs. Leah paused, listened, then dropped both pills into her mouth, the bitterness coating her dry tongue. "Eat me," she thought. Vodka and gatorade washed the bitterness away.

"You know, Leah, you really have so much going for you. A good college, good grades. You're an attractive girl," Leah's lawyer placed a hand on her knee. His wedding ring winked at her. The leaves of the tree outside his office window swayed like shaking heads. "You just get worked up about this. You might feel better if you just focus on other things and move on," he advised.

From the bottom of the pit Leah heard the voices of the passing students long after they had moved on. Students, strangers, a school counselor, a lawyer, Chelsea, and a judge paraded around the hole. Their shadows contorted on the walls. Leah reached for the bottles.
"Not guilty," they had said. "Not guilty."

The judge sat bloated behind his bench, his flushed cheeks and neck bulging out between the collar of his robes and his beady eyes. His massive throat threatened to swallow the gold crucifix on his necklace. Her lawyer had said he was a good Christian judge. A lawyer who made six figures smiled graciously as he finished working his playground. At the plaintiff's table, Leah's lawyer murmured something but she could not hear it through the blood through her ears. She heard his parents smiling. They were all grins.

Leah drove to campus in a daze, forgot where she parked her car the moment she left it, and stumbled to her dorm. The curtains were shut. She left her vibrating phone on her desk. Her body felt like it would shatter at the spinal cord. Leah picked up her things and wandered outside.

It had started to rain. A deluge of dirt flooded into the pit, pattering over Leah's head and backpack and swollen ankle, burying spilled pills. Bodiless voices murmured incomprehensibly in the darkness. Incessant beeping rang above, but Leah could not hear it, not for the chemicals and numbness filling every synapse of her brain.

Leah saw a lake. There were flitting fish, leeches searching for her toes, her mother reading a Jodi Piccoult novel, wearing something yellow, sun bleached life jackets strewn on a wooden dock, water birds swooping above, admiring their reflections. Waves kissed her calves. Leah saw the lake with her eyes open. She closed her eyes and tears trickled onto her dusty cheeks.

The dirt covered Leah and the pit extended to embrace her. A pale arm extended feebly through the fresh dirt, searching for the surface the way a root searches for depth. Heavy clumps of soil pressed her lungs empty, and when she opened her mouth she inhaled the world. For a moment her white fingers curled over the fresh dirt, blades of a delicate plant just beginning to unfurl.

TARA ROBINSON - FIRST YEAR STUDENT
UNDECLARED

A Fork in the Road

"So what's wrong with me, doc?"

He took a decent drag on his cigar. Clinton imagined his corduroy was probably irrevocably soaked in the layers of smoke and cheap cologne that soak his clothes each session.

"Draw three nude women."

"Excuse me?"

He sat up now that the topic was interesting.

"Or clothed, just draw, paint, write, create something beautiful. It helps sometimes."

"What about nude men?"

"I said something beautiful," he said sitting back with smoke escaping his lips in puffs.

Clinton nodded to the side in a touché attitude. He noticed his shirt in the office's light. It was a bronze color. Which was strange for Clinton because he knew this shirt in the daylight as a mustard yellow. He thought the shirt looked gruesomely bronze. He left still displeased with his shirt's pigment in the daylight. He had only worn the shirt a handful of occasions, but thought about shopping for a new wardrobe.

Clinton left before he had the chance to ask him why exactly three, but that was his prescription.

———

Momo's house was one of those houses that had a distinct house smell. Nothing you could pin down, but you knew that smell was the Cordona household. Sometimes his clothes smelled like it too. Clinton wondered why it's like that. Except Momo's room upstairs, that smelled like skunk, and he didn't wonder why it was like that.

"Puff, puff, pass, motherfucker."

Momo was slung on a beanbag chair that survived several childhood garage sales to be in the smoke filled room with them. They kissed the joint while Clinton moved to a bag of pills while Momo exhaled, showboating his lung capacity.

"Today's the day, man." Clinton embraced a single pill between his finger and thumb and felt like Jack deciding to climb the beanstalk.

Momo turned and gave a toothy grin. "Ready to go fast motherfucker?"

They said cheers and washed the pills down with a hit from the burning joint. Clinton's heart was clawing at the top of his chest. He read that his heart rate would increase, but he couldn't tell the symptoms of the pill from the ones in his head. He was anxious about the effects the same way a pirate is anxious after three months on a ship with no treasure in sight.

"Hey, you wanna go cook something? I'm not hungry, but if we make food now we won't have to make food when we are hungry. It'll just be there, like magic."

The Cordona kitchen was spacious and open. It had two archway entrances and a wooden chair from Pottery Barn next to the gray granite top island. Momo enjoyed cooking and already had most ingredients for anything in any of his cookbooks. He silently handed them to Clinton. Clinton browsed the grease and oil stained pages, many of them had shaky, handwritten tips or reviews by Momo himself.

"Let's make roast beef."

"You got it, chump." Momo moved to the fridge to exhume a lump of roast beef in a foil tin.

"You just had this ready to go?"

"The holidays are coming up. All the stores are closed then, so I cook most of the day. We can make a few slices though, I'll sauté them."

Momo established a post by the stove, where he positioned a cutting board and onion. He moved the roast to the island. It was cold and hard and smelt like Thanksgiving leftovers. He moved to the silverware drawer and drew a knife for the onions. Clinton stood between the island and the stove not sure where to put himself.

"I'll start cutting the beef," Clinton announced, but Momo met him at the drawer. He looked at Clinton and wrinkled his face.

"Your face is pretty red, I don't trust you with a knife." Momo moved to retrieve a metal, two-pronged fork.

"Here." He started making straight cuts down the roast. "I'll make a few cuts and you can pick them out and season them." He handed Clinton the fork. They both moved to their stations.

———

Shhlk "uh."

Momo glanced up from dicing onions to see Clinton. The roast was in front of him. So was the fork. The fork handle at least. The prongs dived into his chest enough to hold a right angle against his skin.

"Dude," Momo commented.

Clinton turned his head fluidly with the grace of a doe startled from grazing.

"Fork-et about it."

"Dude."

"I'm fine. My job has some decent health insurance, like if you were forked, then we'd be forked. Drug dealers don't have health insurance."

Momo looked at the few drops of blood on the floor by Clinton's feet.

"It makes sense," Clinton continued. "I mean, anyone can do it, be a drug dealer, I mean. Jails are full of people who could do what you do—or I guess they couldn't, but that's just how the cycle goes I guess. And what would they even prescribe to a drug dealer? More drugs? You'd just be stocking them..."

Clinton was amused. Momo's jaw stiffened.

"I mean, its sounds like a neato job, you get to make drugs all day."

"You know, I'm cooking a roast, not meth right now, right? No, I have hobbies."

Clinton's face grew warm.

"That was really offensive to me, man." Momo frowned.

"Sorry."

"*You* were really offensive."

"I don't mean to be anything to anyone."

Clinton moved cautiously to the low-sitting chair, checking to make sure he had a six inch radius for him and his new appendage to move in.

"Does this remind you of a butterfly?"

"Is cutlery your cocoon?" Momo said with his back to his friend.

"Don't take it out, I don't think I have wings just yet." Momo looked over his shoulder to smile back at his friend.

Clinton remembered something and laughed.

"My therapist told me I should paint nude women."

"You're doing that?"

"Well, I don't have any nude women so –"

"You're doing therapy?"

Clinton wasn't embarrassed, but felt like he should be. He wasn't keeping a secret, the appropriate time to tell his friend he was seeing a repair man just never arrived.

"Just once a week, to talk about things. He's pretty cheap, but still good I think. I think he comes to more sessions drunk than I do." Clinton chuckled and braved a glance up to his quiet friend.

Momo slanted his body with his elbow on the counter. He crooked his head. Clinton was a lanky man; he bounced his leg while slouched in the mahogany recline. He wore a gold V-neck, now stained and punctured with a two pronged, silver snake bite, and drippy red venom on Momo's kitchen tile. Momo's brow wrinkled.

"It doesn't look too bad. It's kind of beautiful," he said.

Clinton looked up with wide eyes.

"Take my picture?"

Momo had an old Polaroid camera he found at a thrift store once and told himself he was going to be more artistic with his free time. Clinton hadn't moved, afraid he would disrupt the dust on the chair and ruin the shot. Taking a knee and lining up his shot Momo held the camera steady for a few seconds before pressing the shutter. As the camera expelled the film, Momo ran around the corner to the spare room to place the developing image in a dark habitat.

"I'm going to leave it in here a little while so it shows up for sure."

Momo bounded around the corner with newfound energy. He was excited to see the picture. He thought of it as the Polaroid that launched a thousand Polaroid and he thought of what to capture next.

"Okay." Clinton nodded. Momo walked toward the granite island. Like Arthur, Momo posed with one leg on the back of chair for leverage and pulled on the silverware.

The doctor's eyes were puffy and reminded his client, Clinton, of two ashy, cigarette butts. Clinton's eyes were also only partially lit, but still clearly lit. If the chairs were more accommodating, he would take a very expensive nap. He scratched at the gauze bandages on his chest.

"How are you eating?"

Clinton thought of the tupperware container of a roast beef dinner from Momo. Given with a set of cutlery, missing a fork–funny–and a holiday greeting card from the chef.

"How are you sleeping, maybe I could prescribe something?"

Clinton looked up, disconcerted.

"Kidding." The doctor tapped his cigar on the ashtray. He read all about the occurrence and added a few more ticks to his client's file.

The Polaroid camera left in Momo's spare room barely translated the scene it was sent to capture. The picture it spat out had a heavy gray overtone. The light touching the hilt of the silver made itself visible, and only if you turned the square like a hologram could you see the man it's imbedded in. His shirt was battle scarred–stained and stabbed and still in his closet.

Momo still says it's one of his favorites, though it was also one of his first. When Clinton returned a few days after the ER patched his flat, he found bags of newly procured film.

"How did you stab yourself with that carving fork anyhow?"

"I was distracted." Clinton looked at his doctor.

"Yeah?"

"I thought the roast was beautiful."

Little Masters

Zipping out of the forest, the little black dog hops over the sidewalk and onto the hot tar. The front door is wide open as people walk about and the rickets of spinning bicycle wheels blend with the buzz of cicadas. He sniffs and the air is dry, almost salty. A small puddle of water hugs the curb from last night's rain and he drinks. Hungry, he trots through the threshold of the front door. He passes his lady master's legs in the kitchen as she prepares Caesar salad for the little masters. Sharply turning around the corner, he heads for the basement. A mobile metronome, his four paws patter down the stairs in even tempo, drumming in the cool of the basement that envelops him. In a nearby room, the little masters sit, lemonade in glasses beside them. With a reception of complements and scratches behind the ear, the little black dog joins them, a little master himself.

Hassan and Goat
TYLER BROWER - FIRST YEAR STUDENT
UNDECLARED

Street Market
TYLER BROWER - FIRST YEAR STUDENT
UNDECLARED

Arabian Desert Saudi Arabia
TYLER BROWER - FIRST YEAR STUDENT
UNDECLARED

Sa'ad
TYLER BROWER - FIRST YEAR STUDENT
UNDECLARED

Syrian Refugees
TYLER BROWER - FIRST YEAR STUDENT
UNDECLARED

Expression
BLAKE VAN OOSBREE - SENIOR
STUDIO ART MAJOR

Landmannalauger
KATIE FETERL - SENIOR
ENVIRONMENTAL STUDIES & GEOGRAPHY MAJOR

Let This Be Your Sanctuary
CALEB MERRITT - FIRST YEAR STUDENT
UNDECLARED

Pillar of Salt, Water
CALEB MERRITT - FIRST YEAR STUDENT
UNDECLARED
Photo by Nick Theisen

Orchard Basket
LILY BENGE BRIGGS - SOPHOMORE
ART EDUCATION MAJOR

Serenity
AIMEE CICHON - SENIOR
PSYCHOLOGICAL SCIENCE MAJOR

Solace
MEISHON BEHBOUDI - SENIOR
PSYCHOLOGICAL SCIENCE MAJOR

Sundar
MEISHON BEHBOUDI - SENIOR
PSYCHOLOGICAL SCIENCE MAJOR

Star-Nosed Mole
SAGE MACKLAY - SENIOR
HISTORY MAJOR

Alan
ELIZABETH LUTZ - SENIOR
ENGLISH & SCANDINAVIAN STUDIES MAJOR

Three Hundred Years From Now
ELIZABETH LUTZ - SENIOR
ENGLISH & SCANDINAVIAN STUDIES MAJOR

Daniel's Reading
LESLEY DARLING - SENIOR
SCANDINAVIAN STUDIES MAJOR

Fog on Bay (Three Friends Laughing)
LESLEY DARLING - SENIOR
SCANDINAVIAN STUDIES MAJOR

Water in Three Forms
LESLEY DARLING - SENIOR
SCANDINAVIAN STUDIES MAJOR

SOPHIE PANETTI - SOPHOMORE
HISTORY MAJOR

BLOOD ON THE TRACKS

My fingers are cotton, the words are trying to come out
But all they do is brush against the paper like leaves
Or the hair across the nape of my neck
It's blood work, it's a long and complicated process
That drains me of everything in my veins
And then someone takes it away and analyzes it
For a cancerous word or an infected phrase
That might be surgically removed later
And doused in alcohol to kill the germs,
Kill the words that slip out unintentionally
So I'll sit here with my cotton fingers
And listen to the train whistle outside,
The loneliest sound in the world, the way it
Throws its voice ahead in the darkness
Like it's expecting an answer and getting none.
I'll put my blood work on the tracks
And let the train roll over it sometime like a penny
Flatten it out, start all over with a blank piece of paper
And maybe then I will be able to write.

In the First Degree

"Murder is Sin!"
They hung him.

JUDITH GABRIEL - JUNIOR
EDUCATION MAJOR

They're Wearing My Shirts

I see them on TV, on posters and magazines
They're wearing my shirts
Shirts that speak of freedom
I wonder what that word even means

I heard they celebrate Black History Month
To remember and talk about struggle,
About hardship and how it was overcome
And while they're praising their God for
Leading their people out of the darkness
They're wearing my shirts

They talk about how it is never the survivor's fault
Survivor, what an interesting word, I think to myself
And they claim women can wear whatever they want
Apparently they like wearing my shirts

I see men kissing men and women kissing women
And they're holding signs that speak of equal rights for all
"We are all human", it says on their backs
I remember making their shirts

Freedom, equal rights for all
Those are just words without meaning
Stitch for stitch, hour for hour
I am left wondering how they cannot smell
My blood on their shirts

If I Got a Tattoo

It would be a single
Dot the size of a

.

To remind me
Of my insignificance
In the universe.

ODE TO NICK DRAKE

You for whom the world was too much
Or not enough
Have shown me the narrowness of such thought.

Slipping in and out of shivers,
With strains and pains in my belly,
Purging myself of what I thought was mine,

I listen and learn that all I need is a place to be,
Pink moons, the sun to rise so I can call it beautiful,
The night to fall once more,

And the peace that comes not from having,
But from abiding.

MIA CANNON - JUNIOR
ART STUDIO & RELIGION MAJOR

Installed 3/1/14

Between the very
           Tips of my fingers
           Is the tiny silver
                                    Door knob
                      I turn it to the
Left
                    And then the

                                                        Right
But nothing happens because
The side of
           My nose
Isn't meant to   open.

A poem after Matthea Harvey
MY BEE BROTHER

pretends he has knees. He jealously
stares at me crouching to pet the cat, then
floats around the room and squeezes
through the speaker holes of the record player,
sometimes mimicking The Moody Blues
or the Corelli Christmas Concerto.
He circles my head after I've crawled into bed,
lulling me to sleep with his droning. I dream
of warm days—a hazy heat rising from wheat fields.
His translucent wings filter early morning
light, reflecting it like a prism into
a spectrum of colours.
He mimes a Charlie Chaplin routine, using
an eyelash for his bendy cane.
At other times, his buzzing body beats against
the window, spelling out 'escape'
with his sticky insect prints. I almost
want to set him free, if only to see
what he'd do in winter.

ELIZABETH LUTZ - SENIOR
ENGLISH & SCANDINAVIAN STUDIES MAJOR

HEMLOCKS

I know a place where
ancient hemlocks meet.
Solemnly they stand,
their branches locked in conference.

One says: 'The time will come with the
rising sun.' Another: 'No, with its setting.'
And a third: 'It will come when the sun
shines straight down like a mother
reaching for her child.'

I cast my shoes aside
to walk on holy ground
in this grove where Peace makes his home.

The trees move ever so slowly,
expanding slyly by centimetres,
soundlessly gaining more ground.

Sighing, they seem to say:
'Ten years are as a day.'

Made in the USA
Charleston, SC
15 May 2015